W9-CFV-302

HOW TO HUG
A PORCUPINE

EASY WAYS TO LOVE
THE DIFFICULT PEOPLE
IN YOUR LIFE

SEAN K. SMITH

WITH A SPECIAL FOREWORD BY
DR. DEBBIE JOFFE ELLIS

MJF BOOKS
NEW YORK

Published by MJF Books
Fine Communications
322 Eighth Avenue
New York, NY 10001

How to Hug a Porcupine
LC Control Number: 2015951403
ISBN 978-1-60671-327-3

Copyright © 2009 by Hatherleigh Press, Ltd.

This edition is published by MJF Books in arrangement with Hatherleigh
Press, Ltd.

www.hatherleighpress.com

Printed in the United States of America.

MJF Books and the MJF colophon are trademarks of Fine Creative
Media, Inc.

QF   10 9 8 7 6 5 4 3

CONTENTS

PART IV
THE PORCUPINE
WITHIN US ALL 121

FOREWORD
By Dr. Debbie Joffe Ellis

This book is a powerful tool.

In fact, it is a tool so powerful that, if we practice its recommendations, it can lead us towards harmony, compassion and a better world.

How?

This book reminds us that we humans have the capacity to create our attitudes and emotions, as well as our actions. If we choose to, we can maintain inner peace despite difficult outer circumstances. We can prevent unnecessary suffering.

If you allow your quills of judgment to turn inwards and pierce you, this book can help you to foster self-acceptance. If you make yourself angry at others who prick you by acting in harmful and provocative ways, the strategies offered in this book will enable you to calm and stabilize yourself. And if you mistakenly allow yourself to be pierced by others, the wisdom of the words in the book reminds you not to take it too personally!

With thoughtful, easy to follow strategies, *How to Hug a Porcupine* shows you how to embrace the Porcupine tendency, while still respecting the quills. You can learn to unconditionally accept yourself as well as others.

The brilliant pioneering psychologist, Albert Ellis PhD, taught that no one can upset us unless we allow them to. Instead we can choose to think rationally, feel calm, and act with consideration, kindness and empathy. We can learn not to think and act irrationally and not to automatically stick our quills out during threatening or provocative situations. Even if the Porcupinely-acting person who you are dealing with resists, your open-hearted approach will not be wasted. Every time we practice kindness, compassion and unconditional acceptance of others, we are reinforcing it within and for ourselves.

How to Hug a Porcupine makes change for a lifetime possible. This is a book that can be picked up, enjoyed and implemented at any time. In fact, it will benefit us tremendously to consult it regularly. We all benefit from reminders, and repeating these exercises will erode persistent negative tendencies. Keep practicing these principles over and over again. Share this book with others, and set an example by modeling its principles.

Life is brief. Time is precious. Wasting it in defense and attack, or in anger and fear, is regretful. Choose instead to practice patience, empathy, compassion, kindness, understanding and unconditional acceptance. Work towards creating greater harmony within yourself and in your relationships, and you will contribute to creating a healthier, saner world.

This book can be used as a dose of preventative medicine, a first-aid kit, and a healing balm, but more than anything else, it is an effective tool for emotional and mental health and well-being. Turn to it to encourage greater awareness of heart and mind.

Use it in your own life, and you will bring stability, peace and joy to yourself, others and the world around you.

— DR. DEBBIE JOFFE ELLIS

A NOTE FROM
THE PUBLISHER

We all know people who are difficult to be around. We may run into them at work, at home, through friends, or simply whenever we are going through our day.

Unfortunately, those "porcupines" are not going to go away!

On the following pages you will find strategies for dealing with those prickly personalities. This is important not only because we simply don't have a choice but to deal with porcupines, but also because it is actually *good* for us to find ways to get along with those who are different from us.

Other people challenge us. Other people improve us. Other people make us better human beings.

— ANDREW FLACH, PUBLISHER

PART I

THE NATURE
AND BEING
OF THE
PORCUPINE

"The supreme happiness of life is the conviction that we are loved — loved for ourselves, or rather, loved in spite of ourselves."

— Victor Hugo

WHY PORCUPINES?

For centuries, cultures from around the world have used animal characteristics to identify and describe human personality traits. In Native American culture, for example, everybody in the community must undergo a mystical rite of passage to identify their animal spirit. This animal then becomes part of their name (examples include "Sitting Bull," and "Little Turtle"). The Chinese Zodiac assigns one of 12 animals to every year, and an individual's personality is believed to be reflected in the attributes of the animal that was appointed the year that one was born. The animal characters in Aesop's fables embody different attributes of human behavior, and their stories and predicaments offer lessons on human nature. Today, expressions like "stubborn as a mule," "wise as an elephant," and "sly as a fox" are still sprinkled throughout conversation.

Whether these expressions, stories, or themes are accurate or not, the way mankind draws links between animal behavior and human behavior reveals a great deal about our struggle to understand ourselves, and each other. This book seeks to help you, the reader, understand and cope with a certain type of person: those individuals who are difficult and challenging. We call these people "porcupines."

Why? To answer that, we need to look at the actual behavior and habits of the porcupine.

THE PORCUPINE IN NATURE

Porcupines are rodents whose coats feature modified, spiny hairs known as quills. These quills are embedded in the skin, and a single porcupine may have over 30,000 quills in his coat. There are 27 species of porcupine, divided into two families: those found in the Old World (Europe, Asia, and Africa) and the New World (the Americas and Australia). Porcupine ancestors date from 30 million years ago. Old World porcupines live on the ground, while New World porcupines are avid tree-climbers. Although some species of porcupine eat small reptiles and insects in addition to a diet of bark, roots, fruit, meadow grass, and tubers, most species of porcupines are strictly herbivores (they eat only vegetables). Unlike most herbivores, who have to seek safety in numbers, the effectiveness of the porcupine's quills as a defense against predators allows it to lead a solitary life.

Even today, porcupines are generally misunderstood. Contrary to a legend which dates back to the Greek philosopher Aristotle, porcupines cannot throw or fire their quills. Nor are their quills poisonous. Their name itself is a misnomer; it derives from the Latin words *porcus* and *spina*, which together mean "thorny pig"—porcupines are neither thorny, nor are they related to pigs (they are, in fact, most similar to beavers in habitat, diet and temperament).

Porcupine babies, called porcupettes, are born with soft, pliable quills. Within a matter of hours, these harden into defensive weapons.

THE PORCUPINE, THREATENED

When porcupines are threatened, tiny muscles at the base of each quill tighten, causing their quills to stand up and the porcupine to appear much larger than it really is. Then the porcupine will rattle its quills, grunt, growl, and stamp its feet, all in an effort to scare off its attacker. If the predator persists, the porcupine will turn its back, raising its tail and crouching defensively. Finally, the porcupine will charge backwards, whack the predator with its tail or throw its body at its attacker. This often leaves a handful of quills embedded, painfully, in its opponent. Over time, the quills can work their way into the flesh of the attacker and cause infection.

Despite its unappetizing quills and highly developed counter-attack, the porcupine is still vulnerable to larger, carnivorous predators. One predator, the American fisher, has evolved a technique for getting around the porcupine's quills; it flips the porcupine onto its back, exposing its tender—and undefended—underbelly.

HOW ARE PEOPLE LIKE PORCUPINES?

Human porcupines would probably be indistinguishable from anyone else, except for their reaction to any kind of threat or incursion. It's then that, like the porcupine in nature, they puff themselves up to try to scare off their adversary.

Unfortunately, this defensive behavior in the human porcupine is "too little, too late" in many ways. That is, the human porcupine only reveals himself when you've already stepped into his bubble—and he is already on the defensive. How do you make up for encroaching on his territory, fix the situation, and determine the best way to avoid future confrontation?

Learning more about the human porcupine, and adapting your behavior, is the first step.

PART II

A BASIC GUIDE TO
UNDERSTANDING
PORCUPINES

"Love one another and you will be happy. It's as simple and as difficult as that."

— Michael Leunig

What follows are some specific techniques to help you not only survive, but thrive, in your encounters with human porcupines. No matter where you encounter a porcupine, whether you are meeting him for the first time or have known her for years, having some reliable strategies in your back pocket can make all the difference in the world. With knowledge and the right attitude on your side, you can not only make the best out of a bad situation, but, with practice, learn how to avoid painful spots altogether. Here are ways to cope with any prickly porcupine with humor, wisdom and practicality.

IIIII

Learn Your Porcupine's Warning Signs

For human porcupines, their "quills" are most often their words, delivered aggressively with fierce language, and often in a loud voice. Learn to recognize these warning signs so that you can be one step ahead when your porcupine gets aggressive.

ffff

Keep Your Quills In

A porcupine's defensive behavior can be contagious. During a disagreement with a porcupine, many people will resort to their own defensive mode. Don't! There is a *very* big difference between trying to understand what is bothering your porcupine and getting into a big fight.

So, take a step back. Take a deep breath. And try again.

Don't let your own quills get the best of you.

////

Respect Your Porcupine's Boundaries

The attack of a porcupine is a last resort of a frightened, cornered creature trying to keep a threat at bay. We should always remember this. Because a porcupine often attacks out of fear, respecting his boundaries will keep him from lashing out.

IIIII

Consider Your Porcupine's Real Needs and Fears

It's important to remember that human porcupines, like porcupettes, are born soft. But bad experiences, fears, and failed relationships have forced them to harden their exteriors and sharpen their quills.

We should keep in mind that a porcupine's quills—the result of past injuries—are a part of who the porcupine is, and they aren't necessarily meant to hurt us. This perspective helps us relate to the porcupine and provides us with the understanding we need to successfully approach her.

//////

Find that Soft Spot!

Even porcupines have soft spots—their belly! Keep in mind that although it may require some close attention and careful strategy, you can find your human porcupine's emotional "soft spot." This will be a topic that, no matter what, brings a smile to his face and makes him feel good whenever he talks about it. It could include a passion, a favorite hobby, or anecdotes about a loved one.

Learn what subjects make your porcupine feel joyful and bring them up—you'll make him feel special and he'll see that you really care about how his life is going.

////

Be Empathic

Loving a difficult person requires a great deal of empathy. Take the time to ask yourself: What is that person feeling? How would I feel if I were inside those quills? What might it be like to deal with someone like *me*? Being responsible and loving towards a porcupine requires emotional maturity and the flexibility to think empathically.

/////

Pay Attention

Pay attention...a lot of attention! If you know your porcupine doesn't like loud music or spicy foods, then exposing her to either one is just asking for trouble. Sometimes, avoiding conflict can make a world of difference!

////

Get to Know Your Porcupine's Likes

Everybody wants to feel special; porcupines are no different. If you know your porcupine likes to relax with a glass of wine after a hard day at work, try to have one ready for her when she gets home. Does your porcupine love to watch Sunday afternoon football uninterrupted? Make plans to steer clear of the TV so he can enjoy this time to himself.

Thinking of a porcupine's needs ahead of time is half the battle. Nothing disarms a porcupine faster than showing her that you care!

fffff

Make Your Likes and Dislikes Clear, Too

Loving a porcupine is a two-way street. It's a process of communication, education and awareness—on behalf of both parties. This means paying attention to ourselves, too. It's our responsibility to make our needs clear to our loved ones, just as it is their responsibility to do the same with us.

Try to "Speak Porcupine"

The best way to deal with a defensive person is to try to get him to talk to you about what gets his quills up. Often the best way to do that is to tell your porcupine what gets *your* quills up. "Speaking porcupine" in this way will show him that you can relate to what it is he is going through and the frustration he may be experiencing.

////

Share with Your Porcupine

Sometimes, exposing your own vulnerabilities can be your best defense. By admitting to your fears and apprehensions, your porcupine will see that you both have weaknesses. This will open up a door of communication.

Sharing will help your porcupine feel safe enough to share her own vulnerabilities with you.

fffff

Keep a Safe Distance

Don't rush towards a porcupine's quills unless you are prepared to handle the encounter (remember, quills can't hurt you unless you run up against them!) Learn how to avoid rushing onto or against your porcupine's quills until you are ready, or until he has calmed down a little.

IIIII

Don't Take it Personally

Chances are, your porcupine's sour mood, though *triggered by* you, has little or nothing to do *with* you. The more you recognize that a porcupine's aggressive behavior is really about your porcupine figuring out her own issues, the more energy you will have to find a solution that works for the both of you.

//////

Avoid Porcupine Strangers so You Can Focus on Your Porcupine

When you are working hard to understand a porcupine who is close to you, avoid those that you don't know. You simply won't have enough energy leftover to handle your porcupine.

So, step one: *avoid porcupine strangers if you can.* If you are caught in a sneak attack (these porcupines include an angry driver you encounter in traffic, or the surly store attendant who is really having a bad day), do your best to ignore their bad mood. *Save your own energy for the porcupines closest to you!*

/////

Deflect an Attack with Kindness

Porcupines attack when they feel threatened, so in order to deflect that defensiveness, try a little kindness instead. By using kind words and expressing a generous and caring attitude, we can defuse the porcupine's apprehensions.

Once he knows you're not a threat, your porcupine will retract his quills and peace can be restored.

fffff

Use Your Porcupine's Name

Everybody is calmed by the sound of their own name. In soothing tones, reassure your porcupine it's going to be all right.

IIII

Plan Ahead

As with most things in life, it helps to be prepared. Before a potential confrontation, decide how you are going to deal with your porcupine and stick with the plan. Having a course of action will help keep you from becoming defensive, too.

HHH

Don't Get Angry

Patience is a virtue. So is understanding. Dealing with a porcupine requires a great deal of both. Resist the temptation to get angry and, instead, approach any confrontation or dilemma with patience and understanding above all else.

////

Don't Get Frustrated

Avoid bringing your own issues "into the ring" with your porcupine. If you do, you risk becoming very frustrated, and frustration means your porcupine's gotten you hooked—in other words, it is just a matter of time before you start acting as out of control as your porcupine.

So take a deep breath and rebalance. Let your porcupine rant—you've got calm and wisdom on your side.

IIIII

Be Thick-Skinned—and Cold-Blooded!

If you are thin-skinned, you will feel every prick of your porcupine's anxiety. Try to be thick-skinned instead. And don't react off-the-cuff. Instead, go slow. Be a tortoise! Your porcupine will burn through her energy quickly, and once he does, you will be on top. Slow and steady wins the race!

fffff

Stay in Control

The stresses, anxieties and bad habits you bring to any encounter with your porcupine are a huge factor in determining how things will work out between the two of you. Remember, your relationship with your porcupine is a two-way street, and you must be a careful negotiator. How you behave, how you speak, react—even smile—can shape the outcome. So, no matter what, stay in control, and don't let your emotions get the best of you.

///////

Stop!

All right, so you are locked in an angry phone conversation with your porcupine. You're each saying things you don't really mean. What should you do?

STOP!

Would you run at a bull waving a red flag? Practice your backstroke in a pool filled with piranhas? No. So why would you go *mano a mano* with a porcupine? If your porcupine is backed up, quills quivering, back off.

Pause and take a moment. Wait until things calm down before continuing.

ffff

Get Advice

One of the best resources for help dealing with difficult or defensive people is—well, other people! Ask friends, co-workers, or neighbors for their perspective. Chances are, each and every one of them has a porcupine in their life. Talking will help you get some things off your chest and perhaps provide you with some strategies, too.

//////

Let Your Porcupine Vent

Everybody needs to vent. So let your porcupine rave if she needs to. In fact, encouraging her to "get it all out" can be an important first step towards change. After all, part of your porcupine's reason for being so spiny could be because she hits a roadblock whenever she has to express her feelings. It can be frightening to engage in a dialogue with someone else when you don't understand emotional language. So help her learn by encouraging her to get everything off her chest.

Remember: you can help. Your love and attention are the crucial first steps to calming your porcupine.

/////

Give Your Porcupine Time

Your porcupine's needs and fears go way back. Uncovering them and dealing with them is a time-consuming process. Don't rush things. Take the time that is needed. Your patience will be reassuring.

///

First Deal with Your Porcupine's Feelings... Then with the Problem.

Too often, we focus on behavior, instead of the motivations *behind* that behavior. This is a crucial mistake, for it's in fact the motivation behind action that most needs to be addressed.

When confronting your porcupine, consider his motivation first. Was he feeling afraid prior to acting out? Is so, what made him feel that way? Thinking along these lines will help you ascertain how you can make him feel less threatened in the future.

Don't forget: the porcupine's defensiveness is an *emotional reaction;* defuse the emotions and you'll defuse the reaction.

/////

Make Your Porcupine Feel Safe

The best way to get your porcupine to retract her quills is to reassure her that she can trust you. Communicate with your porcupine openly, honestly, and empathically. This will help her understand that if there is an issue, that its roots must lie elsewhere.

Remind your porcupine that she is safe with you.

////

Be Specific

Usually when we generalize about another's behavior ("You're always late!" "You never tell me how you feel!"), it's because we're missing the point. It's easier to tackle your porcupine's issues if you don't speak in grand, sweeping terms. Instead, try being more specific. What has your porcupine done that bothered you? Start with that. Be clear about why and how it bothered you. Feel free to use examples, as long as you don't get critical.

Now, it may be impossible for your porcupine not to feel defensive in this situation. But being specific and concise about how a given exchange made you feel will give your porcupine plenty to chew on. Your clarity will limit your porcupine's reaction.

/////

Think: Compromise!

Any heart-to-heart with your porcupine involves emotional work on your part. This is a good thing. A relationship that requires effort on the part of only one party is not a true relationship. For better or for worse, this means that you'll have to make some compromises. A compromise might mean making some changes to your own behavior. This will communicate to your porcupine that you are as good as your word, and that you are claiming responsibility for your 50% of the relationship.

IIII

Ask, Don't Assume

Fears and phobias are matters of perspective. So if you are unsure about where your porcupine might be coming from, don't make the mistake of coming to the table with assumptions about what's driving her behavior. Instead, allow her to explain her behavior in her own words. She will be far less defensive (your curiosity is a good thing) and you might just learn something!

Don't Blame

Nothing brings out the porcupine in each of us faster than being blamed. This is because blame implies that one person has to accept sole responsibility, and this, in turn, eliminates any chance for understanding and compromise. To a porcupine, blame is the opposite of trust and communication. For this reason, blame is one of the things porcupines fear most.

So, when confronting your porcupine, avoid blaming him. This means never using "you" or "your" ("when *you* did this," etc); otherwise he will get defensive immediately. *Be very specific about how your porcupine's behavior affects you, but be expressive about your feelings, and don't place blame or pass judgment.*

IIIIf

Don't Try to Win

There are no winners and losers in a relationship. The same goes for discussions with your porcupine. If you're trying to "win," you're sure to lose.

This doesn't mean that there is no such thing as a "victory" when it comes to relationships with porcupines. Any discussion that promotes honesty, openness and a willingness to talk and change, is a "victory" for you and your porcupine. After all, you are a *team*.

////

Respect the Porcupine,
if not the Behavior

Anyone approaching a human porcupine has to be properly prepared. An essential part of that preparation is the ability to differentiate between your porcupine and his behavior. They are not the same!

While we may not always agree with what our porcupine does, we should never lose sight of why we care for him. We can disagree with or be hurt by our porcupine's behavior, but the porcupine remains front and center in our concerns. We may be disappointed by the deed, but we cherish and respect the doer.

Show care and respect in all your interactions with your porcupine.

IIIII

Don't Be Manipulated

When cornered, who hasn't been defensive, blamed someone else, lied, or created a diversion? This strategy is, unfortunately, human nature, and this means of behavior is especially common in porcupines. So, when dealing with your porcupine, be prepared for psychological strategies you haven't faced since the playground. *"I'm* difficult? What about *you?"* (This kind of cyclical argument really isn't all that different from "I'm rubber and you're glue"). When this starts, be ready for it, and resist. Don't let your porcupine pull you into this counterproductive back and forth. These tactics are fear-filled ways to dodge the question, and they will get you nowhere.

Instead, stay calm and in control.

/////

Set an Example

This is another way of saying that, when dealing with your porcupine, you need to set a good example. So, just as you should avoid being defensive, you should also try to be as communicative, understanding and generous as you'd like your porcupine to be.

Setting an example shows that you are committed to change for the both of you.

MMM

Think: Socrates

The "Socratic method" of teaching (named after the Greek philosopher Socrates) depends not on lectures, but questions. By asking the right questions, you can lead porcupines around to your point of view... and make it seem like they got there all by themselves!

Instead of railing about your porcupine's behavior or reactions, ask her for his version of things. Questions like: "What did it feel like when you did this?" or "How did you feel when this happened?" show that you are paying attention (this will be welcome), and, by not limiting the discussion to your take on things, you will encourage him to open up. The next thing you know, the two of you will have revealed aspects of your porcupine's personality that may not have been known to either one of you.

Be as Good as You Can Be

As should be clear by now, dealing with your porcupine will require your very best effort. You will need to be patient, kind, and loving. You will have to be generous, understanding and empathic. In short, to love a porcupine, we must be the best that we can be.

Don't Be Dismissive

It's not your place to agree or disagree with someone else's feelings. So don't dismiss your porcupine's fears, anxieties or concerns. If she feels them—so much so that it affects their behavior—then those feelings must be respected, and dealt with.

Don't Demand

Your way of dealing with a certain situation may not be right for your porcupine, and you must accept that. In other words, don't confuse "we're sharing" with *demanding* that your porcupine share. Solutions may seem crystal clear to you—but that doesn't matter. *What matters is what is best for your porcupine. Accepting this limitation is essential to finding a way to successfully communicate with your porcupine.*

Don't Interrupt

Interruptions are power-plays. They're ways of suggesting that what you have to say is more important than what someone else has to say. This can be particularly dangerous when it comes to dealing with a porcupine—not to mention inconsiderate.

Let your porcupine speak. Be polite and hold your tongue until it is your turn to share.

///////

Talk, Talk, and More Talk...

Let your porcupine speak and encourage them to keep speaking by asking questions. A talking porcupine is too busy thinking and feeling to get defensive. Even better, a talking porcupine will give you clues about what makes him tick. You can use this information in the future to relate even more fully to your porcupine.

/////

Accept Responsibility, Then Apologize

Apologies can be suspicious. After all, there is really no commitment behind the words, "I'm sorry." What's really required of an apology is responsibility. That is, we need to first show that we understand what we did or said, and then "own" up to it. Then, and only then, can we give an apology that is truly heartfelt. We may have to face some consequences as a result, but meaningful apologies are the only way to move forward.

///

Communicate Your Needs Clearly

You can't accuse your porcupine of "stepping over the line" if you've never taken the time to draw that line. In other words, until you clearly state your needs or boundaries, your porcupine cannot respect them. The first step is yours: state your limits.

MMT

Abandon the Useless Ambition
to Be Right

No one is right all the time. In fact, most of us aren't right much of the time. Imperfect as we are, we nevertheless take great pride in suggesting to those around us that we have everything in working order—and we further insist on our own perfection by declaring that the problem isn't with *us*, it's with *someone else*.

This kind of defensive thinking is a recipe for disaster when it comes to your relationship with your porcupine. Remember: there's plenty about ourselves for each and every one of us to work on and change; plenty of bad habits to overcome.

Stay humble. Obsessing about being "in the right" will lead nowhere.

/////

Be a Good Companion

The greatest gift you can give your porcupine is the sense that she is not alone. If she is facing a tough time or is confronted with something she's not prepared for, let your porcupine know you'll always be there to help her. This will give her the reassurance she needs to deal with difficult issues and will strengthen the bond you have with her.

Remember: you are on the same team!

PART III

WHERE
PORCUPINES
DWELL

"I always prefer to believe the best of everybody, it saves so much trouble."

— Rudyard Kipling

We've laid out some general strategies for loving your porcupine. Now it's time to get much more specific. A porcupine's behavior changes with his or her environment, so the right way to deal with a porcupine at work, for example, is very different from coping with a porcupine at home.

In this next section, we will offer strategies aimed at porcupines in their various surroundings.

PORCUPINES AT WORK

Monday through Friday, most of us spend more time with our co-workers than we do with family and friends. That can make going to work extremely interesting... and potentially exasperating.

Why? Because it's the rare workplace that doesn't have a porcupine or two among its employees. These include the shouting bosses, chronic complainers, non-communicative co-workers and those pessimists who seem incapable of seeing the upside of anything. So what do you do when it feels like a workplace porcupine is making every working hour miserable? How do you handle a porcupine who you have to work with, like it or not?

Don't give up. There are ways to make the workplace more manageable, so you can enjoy your job—and even the people you work with—again.

//////

Stay Firm

It is the nature of a porcupine, as we have seen, to escalate disagreements into full-blown conflicts. Most often, this occurs when your porcupine feels he needs to defend his position. It follows that, when your porcupine is most defensive, it probably means it is because you've hit a nerve. In other words, you have raised a workplace issue that needs to be addressed.

So the next time the boss is shouting and his quills are up, don't back away! If your complaint or concern is legitimate, then you have every right to air it. What's more, you have a responsibility. No matter how high the noise level gets, if you are in the right, stay firm.

////

...But Don't Be Stubborn

Remember to be firm, not stubborn. Firm-ness means using all your diplomatic skills to find a way around your porcupine's defenses to a solution that will work for everyone (not just you). If you are steadfast, confident, an open-minded to all possible solutions, you will not only survive the encounter, but you will also provide your porcupine and your co-workers with an excellent example of the best way to be considerate towards each other.

IIIII

Ask Good Questions...

What is a good question? Well, if your boss explodes when you mention a minor problem, it may be because a bigger issue is looming, such as a deadline. Set the small stuff aside and get to the heart of the matter with a smart question. Why not say, "You seem anxious about the deadline. I am, too. What can I do to get us back on schedule?"

A direct question can cut through your porcupine's anxiety and help the two of you move forward.

////

... And Stick with the Topic

Once you ask the question, porcupines, being true to their nature, may give you a defensive, accusatory answer. Remember: stay firm. Fight the urge to get defensive in your own right. Instead, ask another question. It will soon be apparent that you are trying to help—not accuse or expose—and any good boss will soon recognize this and back down.

A good question, posed carefully, will lead to a good solution.

Listen

By listening, you are transformed from a potential adversary to an ally. By listening, you become someone to be trusted. By listening, you cease to be part of the problem and become, instead, someone who has the information to offer a solution.

/////

Try to See Things Through Your Porcupine's Eyes

Chances are, your porcupine's anxiety is legitimate. Once again, your empathy is your best strategy. Try to imagine how you would feel, whatever the challenge. Share that feeling with your porcupine. When she understands that she's not alone, her defensiveness will lose some of its steam.

/////

Be Supportive

Workplaces and jobsites can be fiercely competitive environments and bring out the worst in any porcupine. Avoid repeating a pattern of accusations followed by self-defense. Instead, use empathy, firmness and sensitivity to defuse workplace competitiveness. This is the best way to move beyond combative behavior and step into a new, more fruitful, mode of co-existing.

Look for Common Outside Interests

There is a good reason for holiday events, bowling teams or company picnics—they help employees meet and get to know one another. So, if your company doesn't have extracurricular events such as these, plan some. Go see a ballgame, relax at a local park, or catch movies and a coffee on a Friday after work. Odds are, you will find that you share many things with your co-workers. By discovering and sharing these in an informal setting, you will be paving the way for more successful, efficient encounters in the future, and you will be building the trust necessary for cooperation.

When conflict arises, interpersonal tools can really help. Work to know more about your co-workers.

////

Let's Make a Deal

Negotiation is a fine art. To truly negotiate, the disputing parties must understand each others' needs and demands, avoid getting emotional, and really concentrate on the facts of the matter. This is key in dealing with porcupines.

So, go ahead! Make a deal with your porcupine.

Be Strong Enough to Admit When You Are Wrong

Admitting fault (which is not the same as apologizing) is a healthy, essential emotional act. By "owning" your actions, you will be setting an example for your porcupine to do the same. If there is no shame in admitting fault then there is no fear of blame, and this gives your porcupine one more reason to feel at ease with you.

PORCUPINES AT HOME

Family life is the building block of society, the primary arena of social interaction. In this way, life at home can provide us with the tools we need to prosper as we grow, or cripple us with insecurities and bad habits. It is within the family network that we learn who we are and how to deal with others.

Family life, therefore, is ground zero for learning how to deal with your porcupine. We all must deal with difficult spouses, problem children, or grouchy parents. How we do so will help shape the quality of our daily lives.

Here are some hints.

YOUR PORCUPINE SPOUSE

Living with a porcupine spouse can be particularly difficult. Not only do we live with our spouses and share our lives with them, but they also live in our hearts. This means their prickly quills can really hurt. These kinds of injuries not only tempt us to act defensively—releasing our own inner porcupine—but also cause a lot of damage to our relationships in the long term. The good news is, with preparation and patience we can protect ourselves and start working on finding solutions so that life with our porcupine can be enjoyable again.

In this section we lay out some ways to deal with your prickly spouse while still loving them as they are. With these tips, you can build a closer relationship and your porcupine spouse may even let down his guard!

fffff

Shed Some Light on the Problem

A common element in advice for dealing with human porcupines is *rationality*. The porcupine's defenses are triggered by passion and irrationality; shed some cold, hard light on the situation, and you take away some of the justification for your porcupine's reaction.

By calmly and raionally analyzing the situation that is unsettling your porcupine, you will go a long way towards defusing his orneriness.

///*

To Love Your Porcupine,
You Must Love Yourself

Your confrontation with the porcupine within you will better equip you to deal with the porcupines in your life. How?

First, it will help you build up emotional muscle. See it as a sort of training camp before the big game.

Second, it will make you more empathic. Having dealt with your own fears, you'll know how hard it can sometimes be to confront the weakest parts of yourself. It will enhance your patience.

Third, it will allow you to lead by example. Your courage and clarity will be inspirational to the porcupines in your life.

IIIII

Call it a Disagreement

Instead of calling it an "argument," try calling it a "disagreement." After all, the word "argument" has no promise of an end point; it implies a never-ending battle of words. The word "disagreement," however, contains the possibility of a solution in its very definition: "agreement." Instead of being viewed as a point of no return, a disagreement can be viewed as a temporary stage or a stepping stone on the way towards eventual accord.

IIIII

Recognize and Avoid Stalemates

Work *together* towards a solution. This will require calm, rational communication. Begin by isolating the issue at hand, striping all your emotional reactions away from it, and then get to the heart of the matter. Avoid accusation, crying, cajoling, guilt-tripping, or any other stalemates. Focus on cooperation.

////

Carefully Choose a Time to Talk

It is crucial that conversation does not take place in the middle of a fight. Instead, schedule a time to have a family meeting, or a one-on-one, about the issue. Then, in calm, empathic terms, ask your porcupine what is bothering her.

Be warned: porcupines, being the defensive creatures that they are, will expect defensive denials and illogical counter-accusations from you. But don't give in! Resist the temptation to play the porcupine's game. Instead, in soothing tones, continue to work at unearthing the problem.

Chances are, once you know what's really going on, a solution won't be so hard to find.

It is key to begin by carefully choosing an ideal time to communicate, so you can take all the time you need.

////

Suggest Alternatives

Let's say that, after talking, you and your porcupine come to the conclusion that she needs some time alone. Now it's time to find a solution that will work for the both of you.

Explore ways in which she can be helpful and participate around the house that doesn't conflict with her "alone time." This might include doing the dishes after the kids are in bed, or walking the dog after she has gotten to relax on her own. In this way, your porcupine can still participate, while getting the time she needs by herself.

////

Work Together

Once you have come up with a plan, be sure to execute it.

After your porcupine has shared his feelings with you, he needs to know that you are partners. Show this is true by carefully working together so that your porcupine will see that his new and improved behavior is supported, and appreciated, by you. The best way to show this is through action.

So put a plan to work—together.

Be Persistent and Consistent

There is nothing more confusing than resolutions that only last a day or two! Be persistent and consistent. Diets, the Egyptian pyramids, and healthy relationships have one thing in common: they all take time.

Be a Role Model

Set a good example for your porcupine as well as the other members of your family. Your willingness to talk openly about relationships, and to accept criticism of your own behavior, will help shape how your porcupine learns to handle uncomfortable situations.

Hang in There

At times, it may feel like you are the only one who is really trying. But know that your porcupine is always watching. Demonstrate your love by practicing patience and empathy and by being supportive. Love is what will teach your porcupine to keep his quills down.

Just when you are about the give up... your porcupine will surprise you.

/////

Play Together

Don't get stuck in a rut. Play together! This is the quickest way to beat grinding routine. This can mean a family vacation, a neighborhood game night, an outing to the movies, or a barbecue. By stepping out of the hum-drum, your porcupine just might have so much fun that he or she forgets all about those quills!

ffff

Stop and Smell the Roses

In times of stress, taking the time to enjoy the little things is more important than ever. Worry can turn anyone into a porcupine, so remember to set aside your concerns for a few minutes every day in order to enjoy something small and simple. This is also important to keep your own energy up so that you can deal with your porcupine.

/////

Keep Your Sense of Humor

Sometimes, this may seem like the hardest thing in the world! But don't give in to a snarly mood. Try not to get too frustrated when it seems your porcupine has a difficult time changing. Instead, try to see the humor in the situation... people are curious creatures, after all.

Laugh, Don't Yell

If a fight is looming, try to steer the course away from harsh words. As we've learned, the act of yelling is one that is chock-full of fear. Laughter, on the other hand, is filled with confidence, assurance and vitality.

So try something funny...just for fun. It might be just the breath of fresh air that you both needed.

"Love is an act of endless for-
giveness, a tender look which
becomes a habit."

— PETER USTINOV

/////

Take a Rain-check

If the timing is not right (you're exhausted from work, the baby's crying, or the pasta is boiling over), be flexible and table your scheduled discussion for another time. This will defuse some of the passion from the moment and give you both a chance to reflect on the disagreement. There is no reason to push the conversation when the mood isn't right. Still, be sure to reschedule promptly for a time that works for you both.

YOUR PORCUPINE CHILD

Nowadays, with text messaging, instant messaging and on-line chatting, our children are preoccupied with relationships and social issues long before they have a firmly established sense of who they are and their values. It is the responsibility of parents to make sure that children develop a strong sense of self and don't squander it on frivolous and sometimes dangerous digital exchanges. With the barrage of distractions our children face today—video and computer gaming, films with age-inappropriate language or subject matter, instant communications and a raft of consumer goods being marketed directly to them—it is essential that parents rise to the challenge.

Despite today's cyber-challenge, in many ways the porcupine child of today is no different than the porcupine child of ten years ago. Consistency, honesty and clarity are still vital parenting skills. Here are some ways to be a good parent when your child gets prickly.

Explain Your Values

Too often, our moral values emerge after the fact, in a sort of default mode. For example, we don't inform our children we don't accept lying until they are caught in a fib. Needless to say, it's too late at that point.

Be forthright and clear about your family values—especially in regards religious faith, tolerance of others, and issues like honesty, trustworthiness, and generosity. This will make it easier for your child to understand the next time you offer her a lesson, and, ultimately, will help her determine what's right and wrong on her own as she grows.

////

Explore Your Values

Part of communicating your family's values to your children is discussing them—in some cases, even defending them. This is an important step in your porcupine child's moral development, as well as your growth as a parent. When your child asks, "Why?" you should either have an answer or be willing to search for one. Sometimes there is no easy answer, but by sitting down with your child and talking through a situation with him, you can teach him a better path towards respecting your family's values and those of others.

////

Stick With the Subject

Porcupines (both the little ones with quills and the larger ones with attitude) depend on distracting others as a form of self-defense. What are accusations and explanations but ways of shifting attention away from the offending behavior and onto something or someone else? That's a classic distraction technique! Don't fall for it. Instead, remember that the best way to bring a disagreement with your porcupine to a swift conclusion is to stay on topic.

Never let yourself get distracted.

Don't Lecture

Explain. Explore. But don't lecture. In dealing with porcupine children, you are attempting to draw their feelings out into the open. A lecture will shut them up. Instead of giving a speech, use a conversational tone which invites participation.

////

Be Vulnerable

Many parents feel they have to be fault-less super-beings in order for their children to respect them; in fact, the opposite is true. It is by being vulnerable and by showing your children that you are affected by the same rules, disappointments and conflicts as they are, that you can show your porcupine child that she isn't alone. Show her you struggle, too, and you will show her that you under-stand why she sometimes sticks her quills out. Then you can move to the next step: showing her that there is a better way to go about things than getting prickly.

////

Be as Good as Your Word

It's simple, but powerful.

Conduct yourself as you would have your child conduct him or herself.

//////

Get to Know What Your
Porcupine Likes

Your relationship with your porcupine child requires sharing and exchange. As we have seen, a relationship that is all one-way is not a dialogue but a diatribe—and it's bound to be frustrating for everyone involved.

No parent should expect that his or her preferences should be their children's, too. Instead, expand your mind a little and try to understand your child's likes and dislikes. For example, if your porcupine son likes listening to one particular hard rock radio station, let him put it on the next time you are both in the car. Feel free to comment—you don't have to just grin and bear it! If you like something, let him know. If you don't, let him know that as well. Expressing your likes and dislikes in a calm, unaggressive manner illustrates to your child the right way to communicate—and just might lead to an interesting discussion.

////

Visit Your Porcupine on His or Her Turf

In the wild, the porcupine goes into its defensive posture when its territory is encroached upon. Our children are no different. If a porcupine child's room is "off limits" to her parents, any visit is going to seem like an invasion.

Respect your child's need for privacy and only enter her room if she gives you permission. If she is OK with it, spend time together in her room during homework time. This will help her realize that you are a friend, not an enemy.

Unplug Yourselves

It's difficult to regulate your children's text messaging if you are texting as much as they are! So why not plan non-digital hours or days into your family schedule? You can start out with a "no texting" rule at mealtimes, after 8 on weeknights, or on Saturdays or Sundays. Less time in the digital world means more time in the real world, and more opportunities to get to know one another.

Resist the temptation to use technology to escape a difficult situation.

IIII

Enjoy Yourselves... For Free!

Competing with TV, video games, cell phones, computers, and other means of entertainment can make spending time with your porcupine child a real challenge.

So be sure to turn off the television, the computer, the Wii, and the X-Box every once in a while, and break out a deck of cards or favorite board game. If your kids don't know the rules, teach them poker, gin rummy, war, Old Maid, or any other game you know. Chances are you'll have fun, and get a chance to see a side of your kids you'd miss if you were all staring at a TV screen. What's more, it will be *your* family's fun... home-made, real-time fun that the best memories are made of!

"Love is the condition in which
the happiness of another person
is essential to your own."

— ROBERT HEINLEIN

Listen as Much as You Speak

A verbal exchange in which one person speaks more than they listen is not called a conversation; it's called a monologue. Resist the temptation to listen to the sound of your own voice! Instead, ask questions and engage your porcupine. When he speaks, get him to explain, not just complain. And listen for as long as he needs you to.

THE PORCUPINE PARENT

The relationship between parent and child is a tricky one. As individuals, a parent and their offspring may not always agree, but as family members you want to be there for each other. This dynamic can make for a lot of friction.

The situation is especially difficult when, as adults, we want to be independent, yet still seek to have a connection to our parents. We love our parents, but we can be overly conscious of their faults and shortcomings. We love our parents, but it may seem that the difference between their life experiences and our own is too vast to overcome.

Still, we all want to rise above old habits and establish meaningful relationships with our parents. This can be especially hard with a porcupine parent. How do we learn to live with a porcupine parent that might be grouchy, judgmental, critical, or just about impossible, let alone appreciate him or her? It can seem like a hopeless task. Fortunately, there is a solution.

First, take a deep breath. Now, read on.

//////

Understand "That Was Then, This Is Now"

For most of us, childhood is a time when we develop self-awareness and self-reliance. Often, our growing sense of self collides with our parent's sensibilities, expectations, and values. Although such conflict is often painful, it is vital to attaining independence.

Some children and their parents, however, cannot forgive or forget the specifics of that conflict. Things like screaming fits, slammed doors, or hurtful words continue to sting, even into adulthood.

When dealing with a porcupine parent, remember: that was then, this is now. Our "now" may contain echoes of the past, but it can also be a brand new start. In other words, although we may strive to understand the past, we do not have to be a slave to it.

The direction of our present, and our future, is up to us.

////

Meet Your Parent as a Stranger

Try this experiment. Pretend you are on an airplane, and you have just taken your seat for a transatlantic flight next to an older stranger... in this case, your parent. How would you start a conversation? What might you learn about him or her? How would you relate to one another? Be as specific as you can when you imagine the conversation; think about how, as you discovered more and more about each other, the conversation would start to flow. Maybe you would even make plans to meet again after the trip.

There is no reason that kind of mutually satisfying, mutually engaging conversation can't take place at your kitchen table. There is much about each other that you are your parent don't know; the more you share, the more you may discover you have in common.

//////

Put Yourself in Your Porcupine's Shoes

Sometimes it can seem that, no matter how hard you try, your porcupine parent is still being difficult. No matter what you do, something always seems to be wrong—with your cooking, your child-rearing skills, the way you dress—everything! This can be very frustrating.

Keep in mind that you were once reliant on your porcupine parent; now, that is no longer the case. Your parent may be drawing comparisons—between their parenting and yours, their house and yours, their lifestyle and yours—as a way to maintain their influential role in your life. This isn't malicious; she is just operating the way she used to. Appreciate what she is dealing with. Try to understand why changing might take time for her.

Your calm and empathic manner will defuse most situations.

IIII

Allow Your Parent a Legacy

Everyone, especially a porcupine, has an image of themselves as they wish to be seen and remembered by others. *An amazing dancer. An expert fisherman. The life of the party. A prize-winning baker.*

Let your porcupine parent define his legacy and explore it with you and your children. His concept of himself may not coincide with what you cherish him for. But it is how he thinks of himself and would like to be remembered. Honor this. And think: you might also learn about aspects of your parent's life that you never knew.

///*

Keep Your Porcupine Parent Involved

A parent may be acting like a prickly porcupine simply because she is bored! Involve your parent in your daily life. Invite her to join you on trips to the movies, errands in town, light lunches or barbecues at a friend's or neighbor's house. Let her plan some outings for the two of you as well. If your schedule seems too hectic for her, try to slow down, or encourage her to get involved in other activities. Then, regroup at the end of the day and let her tell you all about what she experienced that day.

ftttt

Calm with Care

Openness trumps defensiveness. Care beats mistrust. Attention cures fear.

By staying present and engaging with your parent, you are communicating love to your porcupine.

PORCUPINES OUT
AND ABOUT

How often have you run across some-one who is clearly having a rotten day, if not a lousy week? These individuals can include a surly phone customer service repre-sentative, a checkout clerk with attitude, or a grouchy waitress.

What is the best way to deal with them? After all, we don't know them that well, and it can be hard to know how much time and energy to invest in negotiating their moods and struggles. But just because we may never run across this porcupine again doesn't mean we shouldn't try to make the best of the situation.

Here are some strategies for making the best of those run-ins with life's unexpected porcupines.

///////

Try a Kind Word

Some days you just don't have to time to really talk to someone and guide them past whatever is bothering them (and, even if you did, some porcupines just stay prickly no matter what).

So, keep things simple, and just offer a kind word. Sometimes, that's all that's needed to change a porcupine's outlook.

fff

Don't Blame Yourself

If a situation quickly becomes awkward when you encounter a strange porcupine, remember, it isn't your fault! The awkwardness is emanating from the porcupine. You are not to blame.

Know When to Walk Away

Being compassionate doesn't mean being a pushover. Your porcupine may have some problems he wants to get off his chest. Encourage him to express it in constructive ways. But if his vocalizations get personal, you have every right to walk away.

/////

Consult a Manager

Asking to see a manager may seem like an embarrassing last resort. But you may, in fact, be providing the porcupine in question with an opportunity: it is quite possible that her employer has needed to address a long-simmering situation for some time now. So, if it seems necessary to you, calmly and politely ask for the manager. With the right attitude, you just might lead all parties involved towards mutual understanding and change things for the better—for good.

PART IV

THE PORCUPINE
WITHIN US ALL

"Make it a practice to judge persons and things in the most favorable light at all times and under all circumstances."

— SAINT VINCENT DE PAUL

It should be clear by now that everyone has an inner porcupine that springs to life whenever we are challenged or criticized—especially when we are faced with a habit or behavior we are self-conscious about.

We all have some aspect of ourselves that we wish could be a little different; some of us wish we were more productive at work, that we went to the gym, or that we kept the living room a little cleaner. These are our sore spots, and, lo and behold, whenever someone brings them up, our porcupine springs into action. Instead of considering someone else's thoughts or conserving our energy, the quills stand up, and our porcupine defends our work performance, physical stamina, or the cleanliness of the living room with fire and fury. By the time our inner porcupine retreats, we have caused a fight, wasted a lot of energy, and moved ourselves even farther from the opportunity to change.

Remember: when it comes to successfully interacting with the porcupines in your life, it is crucial that you start with the one you know best...

YOU.

/////

Be Brutally Honest with Yourself

We can't expect our loved ones to be honest and responsible about their actions if we can't do it ourselves. So take stock of your faults and weaknesses—that's the first step towards change.

IIII

Recognize Your Defensiveness

Everyone manifests their anxieties and defensiveness in different ways. Some people get whiny. Others become short-tempered and irritable. Some find they eat too much, or not enough. Others tune out.

Learn to spot the clues that signal your defensiveness. That way, you can get to the root of what's really wrong, rather than continuing to act out in unproductive ways.

*****

Acknowledge Your Shortcomings

What are you defensive about? Why? These are crucial questions that you may or may not be ready to answer. But you must ask them, if you are ever going to get to a solution. If you need help, ask a loved one, friend or therapist.

/////

Don't Cut Corners

Confronting yourself is the hardest, most essential challenge you will ever have to face. Be kind to yourself during this process, but be honest about what you need to accomplish and commit yourself to the work that needs to be done. Acknowledge your shortcomings. Make a plan to deal with them. And stick with the plan—no matter how much you may try to talk yourself out of it!

A LAST WORD....

You have come to the final page of this little book. We sincerely hope these tips have helped prepare you for dealing with all of the porcupines in your life. Most of all, we hope these words have shown you that all people (even the prickly ones!) need and deserve love. Bring these tips into your own life, and don't be afraid to hug a porcupine!

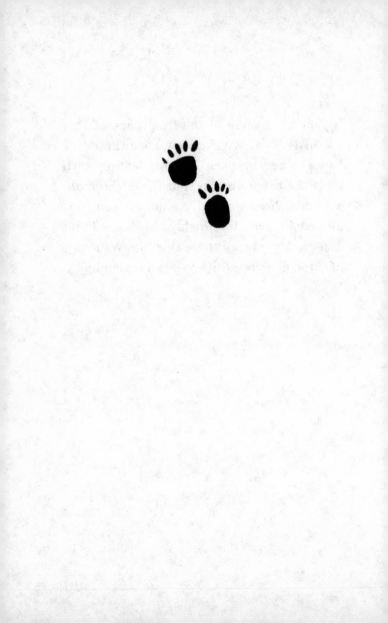